T0276619

LESS

RACHEL AUST

LESS

a visual guide to minimalism

CONTENTS

INTRODUCTION

Before you get too tangled up in decluttering your closets, organizing your schedule, and learning how to keep the mess at bay for good, let's start with the basics. You may be asking yourself questions such as, what is minimalism, exactly? Why is it important? And who is it for? This section will give you an idea how you can fit minimalism into your life regardless of your aspirations, career goals, or family dynamics.

WHAT IS MINIMALISM?

Minimalism is …

… unsubscribing from the idea that how much you own equates to your level of happiness.

… letting go of the unnecessary.

… the removal of distractions.

… a way to reclaim your time.

… an intentional way of living that allows you to identify what's important to you.

… simplicity.

… freedom.

COMMON MISCONCEPTIONS ABOUT MINIMALISM

Novices have so many questions about this lifestyle, and common misconceptions arise regularly in conversation and online. Let's address these before you start down your own minimalist path. The most important thing to remember is that you're shaping your own lifestyle to contain only what you love and enjoy, and there are no hard and fast rules to follow to achieve that.

YOU CAN'T OWN NICE THINGS

This depends on your approach to minimalism. You can be frugal, purchase only second-hand items and cut all your bills to just what you need to survive, or you can restrict your spending to purchase fewer items that are higher in quality. You choose how to invest your money.

MINIMALISTS ONLY WEAR BLACK, WHITE OR GRAY

Many minimalists gravitate to a wardrobe in a restricted color palette for versatility. Working with fewer colors allows more combinations to be created from a smaller number of items. But this isn't a rule. Incorporate as much color into your closet—and your life—as you like.

YOU HAVE TO BE VEGAN TO BE A MINIMALIST

Some minimalists wish to simplify their diet, consume lower on the food chain, and eat food that creates less packaging waste, so they choose veganism. However, diet is definitely a lifestyle choice, and you don't have to go vegan in order to call yourself a minimalist.

MINIMALISTS HAVE TO KNOW THE EXACT NUMBER OF THINGS THEY OWN

A few minimalist bloggers initiated this concept after counting and announcing the exact number of things they own. For some people transitioning to minimalism, this can be a useful approach to help cull items; for others it may feel too restrictive and stressful. The choice is yours.

MINIMALISTS ARE ALWAYS SINGLE

It's commonly believed that you can only be a minimalist if you're single and/or live alone. This is simply not true. You can still apply a minimalist lifestyle to a family household to reap the benefits it provides.

MINIMALISM IS JUST AN AESTHETIC CHOICE

In the last few years, it has become quite trendy to use the phrase "minimalist" in interior design and fashion-marketing pitches. Aesthetic minimalism does exist, but it's actually fundamentally different from adopting a true minimalist lifestyle.

LEAVE A SMALLER FOOTPRINT

You should feel free to follow your own path when it comes to minimalism. It's your own journey. However, one aspect of the lifestyle that appeals to many of its adherents is the reduction of their carbon footprint upon the world. Through minimalism, you'll purchase less, which also means throwing out less later.

DITCH FAST FASHION

Fast fashion is the reason your clothes are on trend and then out of style so quickly, prompting you to buy more to keep up with what everyone else is wearing. New designs are sent to stores weekly, delivering the latest styles to customers. Fast fashion comes at a low price—but at such a cost! The garments are generally made at a lower quality to be sold a cheap price point, so they fit poorly and fall apart quickly. Fast fashion helps creates a cycle of boredom with your wardrobe.

Investing in quality clothing means you'll buy items that will last longer, so you won't continually add cheap apparel to the landfill every few weeks.

MAKE WISER FOOD CHOICES

When it comes to food, if you shop in bulk rather than purchasing lots of prepackaged goods, you'll contribute less plastic waste to the environment.

TAKING IT FURTHER

As an additional step, many minimalists embrace veganism and a zero-waste lifestyle. You don't have to adopt these habits, but you may find them illuminating as you strive to consume less of the Earth's resources.

Vegan minimalists opt to eat low on the food chain. They don't eat or use any animal products whatsoever—no meat, no eggs, no dairy (and no wool or leather, either). Vegans generally prefer to buy fresh produce whenever possible. This means almost all the food they purchase will be used, and if it's not eaten it can be composted.

Zero-waste minimalists attempt to bring next to no waste-creating products into their homes. Some of these include plastic bottles containing commercial cleaning supplies, wrappings and plastic containers for foods, and other short-term disposable goods.

While you may not want to go this far, be aware that your lifestyle as a minimalist can help reduce the amount of waste you contribute to the world's landfills. Remember to shop smart and live intentionally.

MINIMAL CHALLENGE *Recycle a broken item in your home by taking it apart and repurposing it, or using some parts from it, or making some part of it useful again.*

PARE DOWN TO THE ESSENTIALS

This section takes you through the basics. To ensure you don't get overwhelmed and go overboard culling your possessions, you'll begin with the clutter and other items that you don't often use. This will ease you into sorting through everything you own to figure out what's important to you, your family, and your lifestyle, and help you get rid of things you own merely because you forgot you even have them.

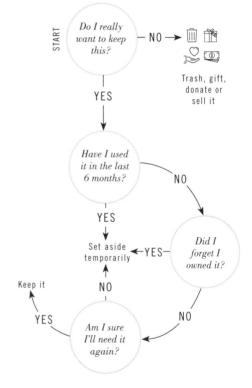

STEP

1

Pick up each item in turn—handling each item forces you to make a decision about it—and ask yourself the following questions.

THE BASIC PROCESS

The basic process of decluttering can begin in an area as small as a single drawer, or as large as an entire room—choose the approach you find the least overwhelming. To begin, you'll need four boxes, bags, or piles. Label them trash, sell/gift/donate, keep, and repair.

If you're serious about becoming minimalist, you should answer the questions honestly and do as the flow charts direct without hesitating.

> *Remember to focus on what you need to keep, not on what you're getting rid of.*

After finishing step 1 with all items, revisit all the things you set aside temporarily. Holding each one in turn, ask yourself the questions in this flow chart.

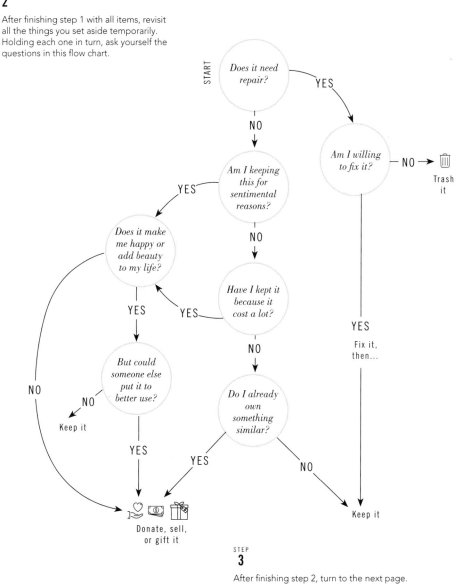

START

Does it need repair?

YES

NO

Am I keeping this for sentimental reasons?

YES

NO

Am I willing to fix it?

NO →

Trash it

Does it make me happy or add beauty to my life?

YES

Have I kept it because it cost a lot?

YES

NO

YES

Fix it, then...

But could someone else put it to better use?

NO

NO

Keep it

Do I already own something similar?

YES

NO

YES

Keep it

Donate, sell, or gift it

STEP

3

After finishing step 2, turn to the next page.

17

25 THINGS YOU CAN TRASH WITHOUT EVEN THINKING

1

Broken appliances or electronics

2

Expired makeup products

3

Old receipts

4

Old notebooks

5

Expired medicine

6

Expired food

7

Kitchenware containers with no lids

8

Broken or dried-out pens

9

Old, unimportant papers and documents

10

Worn-out shoes

11

Unused CDs and DVDs

16

Expired skincare products

21

Purses or handbags you don't use

12

Clothing that doesn't fit

17

Old magazines and newspapers

22

Socks or stockings with holes

13

Old batteries

18

Toys that pets or kids don't use

23

Old, non-functional cookware

14

Unused craft supplies

19

Worn-out sheets and bedding

24

Worn-out towels and bathmats

15

Unfinished projects

20

Unused or broken clothes hangers

25

Mystery keys

TIPS FOR DETACHING FROM YOUR STUFF

Some things are harder than others to separate yourself from, particularly sentimental items, expensive objects, and gifts from loved ones.

There may still be stuff sitting in your "keep" pile that you can detach from, so you need to return to that pile again.

FOOD FOR THOUGHT

As you go through the questions in the decision tree at right, think of these points.

LET GO OF SYMBOLS

An object could be serving as a memory or symbol for some special thing or time in your life. It might even remind you of a person. Remind yourself that the object itself is not that person or time. Take a photo of it if it's something that's not contributing usefulness or beauty to your space, then get rid of it.

BE REALISTIC

Answer honestly: If the item were stolen, would you actually replace it, or do you use it so infrequently that you wouldn't bother buying another one?

SET A TIME LIMIT

By giving yourself a cutoff time to make decisions, you won't spend hours agonizing over whether you may or may not ever wear that random sweater you got as a gift. A time limit will cause you to rely more on your gut instincts.

WEIGH THE VALUE

Are you deciding to keep an item based on its monetary value, or the value that the object itself adds to your life? Consider selling or donating expensive items so that they enrich the life of someone who actually needs them.

LOOK TO THE FUTURE

Think forward in time: Will you actually need this item, or is it just another possession you're going to be lugging around because it's the "norm" or you feel expected to?

Start by sorting out the pricey items and the sentimental objects in your keep pile, then take the following steps to answer the questions about them.

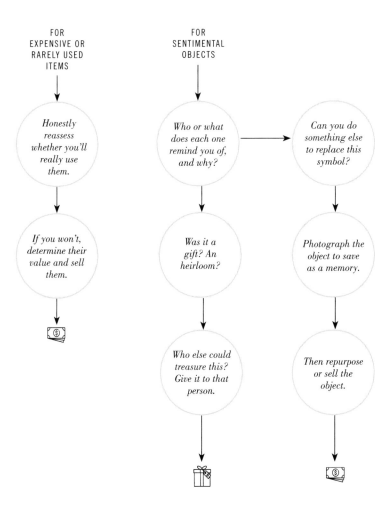

DON'T GET CARRIED AWAY

It feels great to start freeing yourself of the physical objects that weigh you down and don't contribute positively to your life. It's important, however, to remember that you *do* need to retain some possessions to maintain quality of life and keep your home functional. Follow these methods to make sure you're not trashing too much stuff.

MINIMAL CHALLENGE *Don't buy anything at all for 24 hours.*

THINK ABOUT OTHER SEASONS

This is particularly important when it comes to clearing out your wardrobe. What you own should last you through all four seasons of the year, not just the one you're in currently.

DON'T WORRY THAT YOUR SPACE DOESN'T LOOK MINIMAL ENOUGH

You can alter the way you store or display possessions later on, but if you get rid of too many things you use now, you'll end up having to buy them again.

SPACE IT OUT

Don't attempt to get rid of everything in one day. Set goals and small tasks for yourself so you can assess what you need to own.

FINISH WHAT YOU START

Don't jump from room to room or from drawer to drawer when decluttering. Set aside one area to focus on and finish it before moving on to the next.

DON'T COMPARE YOURSELF TO OTHERS

Just because someone else is able to live out of a backpack doesn't make it realistic for you. You may have kids or other family members in your house, or maybe you need particular items for your job. Don't focus on another person's lifestyle.

LET OTHERS DECIDE THEIR PATH

While decluttering you shouldn't be throwing away things that belong to your significant other/housemates/siblings/parents. This behavior will only breed resentment. Respect other people's possessions and wishes.

ORGANIZE

Organization isn't the same thing as minimalism. While it might feel good at first to put all your extra bits and bobs away into pretty matching containers, they're still *there*. Once you actually start to get rid of clutter and release it from your life, the good feeling of owning fewer items and really beginning to live intentionally sets in. Organizing what you have left after that satisfies the desire for orderliness and keeps you aware of what you own.

PLACE ITEMS YOU USE DAILY IN ACCESSIBLE LOCATIONS

This will help prevent you from repurchasing "lost" items that aren't really gone at all.

GIVE THINGS YOU USE LESS FREQUENTLY THEIR OWN "HOMES"

That makes them easy to locate. In a box, in a drawer, in the spare bedroom—these are not exactly good spots to find something. The fewer things you own, the more you can take advantage of the storage spaces in high-traffic areas of your home.

STORE NECESSARY BUT INFREQUENTLY USED ITEMS TOGETHER

These could be seasonal items, such as a winter wardrobe, or tools you don't need all the time but that are still important to own, such as a hammer and screwdriver. Put like items away in one place.

CONTAINERS AND COMPARTMENTALIZING

Use these ideas to organize and store items out of sight—or in plain view.

Foldable storage boxes

You can use these to organize items inside cupboards. Later, as you declutter and no longer need them, break them down flat.

Silverware organizers

No need to reserve these only for silverware! They're a great way to keep jars of spices and other cylindrical objects from rolling around in your drawers.

Mason jars

From stationery supplies to bulk groceries, mason jars—which come in different sizes—are a practical storage option that adds a nice touch to your décor, too.

MINIMAL CHALLENGE *Organize your portable hard drive files.*

Perfection is achieved, not when there is nothing more to add,
but when there is nothing left to take away.

—Antoine de Saint-Exupéry (1900–1944), author of The Little Prince

30-DAY MINIMALISM CHALLENGE

DAY	TO-DO
1	Define your personal style (both your wardrobe and interior).
2	Set aside 20 minutes just for cleaning; repeat daily.
3	Decide on your 20 wardrobe essentials.
4	Declutter your wardrobe and shoes.
5	Declutter your kitchen (pantry and cupboards).
6	Reassess your budget.
7	Clear all bench/table surfaces in your home.
8	Check your bank debits or any old recurring payments (you may no longer need them).
9	Set one long-term goal in each category: health, finance, happiness, and knowledge.
10	Unsubscribe from marketing lists.
11	Digitize as many paper documents as possible.

DAY	TO-DO	DAY	TO-DO
12	Create a planner that works for you (in a notebook or on your phone).	22	Declutter storage spaces (laundry room, garage, attic, etc.).
13	Set three short-term (achievable in 3 to 6 months) goals for your health, finance, happiness, and knowledge.	23	Find 30 minutes in your daily schedule to switch off.
		24	Declutter books, DVDs, CDs, and any other physical media.
14	Set up a direct debit into a savings account.	25	Reorganize your work desk or work station.
15	Sort your inboxes until you get them to zero.	26	Assess which sentimental items you really need to keep.
16	Declutter makeup, skincare, and hair care products.	27	Plan seven days of home-cooked meals—every meal—and make a shopping list.
17	Take all items off the walls and rehang only the important ones.	28	Cull your accessories (sunglasses, watches, jewelry, bags) to the bare essentials.
18	Back up important data, then delete all unnecessary apps/files from your phone and computer.	29	Allocate specific days and times of the week to stretch and practice mindful breathing.
19	Spend a day completely off social media.	30	Set your next goals.
20	Practice mindful breathing techniques.		
21	Social media cull: unfriend/ unfollow.		

DECLUTTER YOUR MIND

A serene, quiet mind is often a pleasant side effect that results from living in a minimalist environment. With fewer visual interruptions, your thinking can become more focused. Decluttering your mind is a great way to reduce stress and make the rest of your day more productive. There are many ways to further cultivate this mindset.

TRY THESE IDEAS TO DECLUTTER YOUR HEADSPACE

Go for a walk

Meditate

Get in touch with nature

Get acupuncture

Practice mindful breathing exercises

Journal

Single-task

Improve your sleep patterns

Watch less TV

Take a long bath

Make sure your schedule isn't overbooked

Swim

Draw

Paint

Sit on a beach

Do yoga or pilates

Log off your computer

MINIMAL CHALLENGE *Meditate for 15 minutes.*

SIMPLIFY YOUR HOME

A simple home, free of excess clutter, unused items, and extra furnishings, cuts down your cleaning time, makes rooms seem more open, and brings more peace to daily life. Simplifying your home doesn't mean having to get rid of everything. *You* set the rules. But you might find it useful to live by this concept: For any item to stay in your home, it must either contribute usefulness or beauty to the space.

APPROACHES TO MINIMALIST DECOR

There are multiple benefits to decorating in a minimalist style. Your home becomes easier to clean. Your space is more appealing to look at. Reducing the amount of stuff you own can even reduce your stress. That said, your digs don't have to look like you've just turned your living room into a favorite Pinterest board. Focus on what matters most to you and what you actually need to get by.

You don't have to own things just because everyone else does. Don't watch much TV? Get rid of it. Don't have enough clothes for a full set of drawers? Don't use a dresser; hang up your clothes instead. We're brought up with the expectation that a section of the house has to look a certain way—your living room should contain a TV, for example, and a bookshelf, a large couch, a coffee table, at least one rug, speakers, and some décor … but if you're using your home differently, you don't need to follow those rules and can instead create a space you truly enjoy.

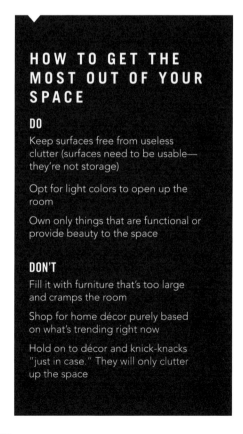

HOW TO GET THE MOST OUT OF YOUR SPACE

DO

Keep surfaces free from useless clutter (surfaces need to be usable—they're not storage)

Opt for light colors to open up the room

Own only things that are functional or provide beauty to the space

DON'T

Fill it with furniture that's too large and cramps the room

Shop for home décor purely based on what's trending right now

Hold on to décor and knick-knacks "just in case." They will only clutter up the space

COZY DÉCOR

Calming.

Comfortable.

Home-y.

Expressive.

1

Select a few, well-chosen accessories to warm up your space.

2

For accessories, avoid hard materials such as plastics and metals.

3

Use lamps to create atmosphere.

4

Stick to soft neutrals for the base color palette.

5

Use lots of plants or art to create a welcoming environment.

HARD-EDGE
DÉCOR

Sleek.

Strong.

Clean.

Refined.

1

Focus on strong lines and stark colors, such as black, gray, or white.

2

Remove or store away all objects that serve no function. Remove as many furnishings as you possibly can.

3

Invite in lots of light.

4

Play with textures, particularly reflective or matte ones.

5

Utilize storage spaces.

FRUGAL
DÉCOR

Upcycled.

Shabby-chic.

Vintage.

Pleasant.

1

Shop second-hand stores (or look online for pre-owned items).

2

Repurpose other furniture pieces for your needs.

3

Repair instead of replace.

4

Take your time searching for quality items, and furnish slowly.

5

Paint pieces to refresh them, and add new hardware, such as knobs or handles.

EVERYTHING IN ITS PLACE

Creating a "home" for your belongings and storing similar items together in the same place makes it much easier for you to find things the next time you need them. This prevents you from having to repurchase items simply because you don't know where they are.

The items you store don't have to be tucked away in the back of a cupboard somewhere. They just have to be accessible to make what you do own as useable as possible. You could have open storage: display a special bowl on a bench or table to hold your keys, wallet, and sunglasses, for example.

Consider storing the following items together.

IN THE CLOSET OR ON A RACK

- In-season clothing
- Shoes
- Bags
- Underwear/pajamas

IN A BOX OR DRAWER

- Art supplies
- Pencils
- Pens
- Journal

IN A TRAY OR BOWL ON A TABLE

- Keys
- Wallet
- Sunglasses/reading glasses

IN A CLOSET

- Linens
- Towels
- Out-of-season clothing

IN CABINETS OR IN DEEP KITCHEN DRAWERS

- Pots and pans
- Lunchboxes/travel food storage
- Kitchen appliances (blender, processor, toaster)

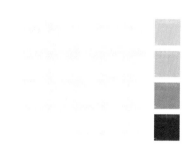

SHELL: Serene, coastal, inviting

COLOR PALETTES

One way to ensure that your home has a unifying theme and doesn't accumulate unnecessary clutter is to pick a color palette for the paint and décor. Selecting the right colors for you (and your family) can create an emotionally healthy home, and a space where you feel comfortable enough to unwind and let your stresses melt away. These nine palettes, consisting of one primary wall color with a number of shades to use for furniture and décor, help create a calming space. Copy them exactly, draw inspiration from them—or come up with your own, of course.

OVERCAST: Tranquil, chic, restrained

CHERRY BLOSSOM: Romantic, warm, charming

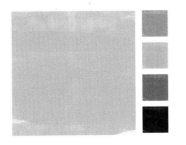

EUCALYPTUS: Calming, natural, rejuvenating

CANARY: Invigorating, uplifting, refreshing

FEATHER: Cozy, quiet, serene

WHEAT: Mellow, soft, charming

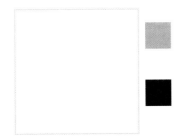

NEUTRAL: Refined, bold, polished

QUARTZ: Delicate, sweet, subtle

THE ONLY 45 ITEMS YOU NEED IN YOUR HOME

1 Bed
2 Sheets
3 Pillows
4 Bedside table
5 Couch
6 Dining table and chair(s)
7 Desk with office chair
8 Mirror
9 Curtains or blinds
10 Food
11 Fridge and freezer
12 Microwave
13 Stove and oven
14 Kitchenware
15 Plates
16 Bowls
17 Cutlery
18 Drinking cups
19 Dish towels
20 Lamps
21 Trash can
22 Trash bags

The sculptor produces the beautiful statue by chipping away such parts of the marble blocks as are not needed—it is a process of elimination.

—Elbert Hubbard (1856–1915), writer, publisher, artist, and philosopher

STRATEGIES FOR DISPLAY

Your home doesn't have to be completely stark and empty to be minimalist. You should feel free to express yourself by keeping objects where you live. Here are some ways to show them off without cluttering up.

Floating shelf

FLOATING SHELVES

Shelves secured to the wall by anchors (a.k.a. molly bolts) are a fantastic way to store your items and get them off the floor or other surface spaces. The ability to hook these shelves wherever you like on the wall means you can create a layout that works best for you, and they look so much neater than standard shelving units.

ITEM CURATION

Displaying just one curated item on a shelf or horizontal surface, rather than surrounding it with lots of stuff, will turn that item into a statement piece, whether it's a single photo or one item that you absolutely love.

So how do you decide what to put on display? Well, that's up to you! You might love changing things around a lot for a visual refresh, or you could just select the items you find beautiful to put out on view. Keep in mind, even if something is a functional item you use regularly, you can feature it as a decorative object, too.

One curated item

MINIMALIST HARDWARE

Floating frames   Floating frames surround the image with glass rather than a backing board, creating less of an interruption in the flow of your wall so it looks larger and the room appears more spacious. These frames are often simple in design and won't outshine the artwork on display.

Wire grids   A wire grid can be a great way to organize your inspirations or mood boards for projects you're working on. All you need is a wire grid from a hardware store and some small pegs or clips from a craft-supply store. Either hang the grid up on the wall or lean it against it a horizontal surface for a more casual look. The benefit of this display system: You can easily and quickly change it whenever you desire. You can also spray paint it any shade you like.

DIY organizer   You can purchase a DIY organizer, or make your own from plywood and hardware for a storage option custom-designed for your belongings. This could be a board that sits in your entry to hold keys, wallet, and miscellaneous items, or a jewelry organizer to keep all your necklaces, rings, and watches in the same place.

Wire grid

MINIMAL CHALLENGE   *Replace a large number of photos with a slideshow in a digital photo frame.*

CREATING SPACES THAT LOOK AIRY AND LIGHT

Air and light not only open up your rooms to make them feel and appear much larger than they actually are, but light, airy spaces bring an intrinsic sense of tranquility. This in turn transforms your home into a place of relaxation and recuperation.

FURNITURE SIZE

Be conscious of the scale of your furniture. If you live in a small place, use small furniture that creates the illusion of space, such as daybeds rather than large lounge chairs, or a narrow bedframe instead of a frame with a solid base. Streamlined furniture with a clean, low silhouette helps a living space look airy.

MIRRORS

Strategically place mirrors in your home where they will reflect the most light and open up the room visually.

LIGHTING

Allowing light into your home is key to making it feel more open. Cooler temperature LED lights can achieve the same at night.

WHITE SURFACES

Opt for white surfaces on cabinets, desks, and tables to make them seem less obtrusive.

WALL COLORS

Neutral or light paint on walls will give the illusion of a space that seems lighter and larger than it actually is.

PLANTS

Plants breathe life into a space, making it feel less stark and look more alive.

WINDOW COVERINGS

Unless your space is very large, avoid heavy window coverings, such as very large drapes. Instead, opt for light, breezy fabrics or sheers, or roller shades that disappear almost completely out of sight when not in use. Vertical blinds are another elegant, minimal-looking option.

LIGHT-COLORED FABRICS

Light fabrics on couches, beds, and cushions keep the visual clutter to a minimum, causing the furnishings to appear smaller so they seem to take up less space.

FLOORS

Light-colored floor coverings cause a space to open up visually. Keep rugs or mats simple in design so they avoid becoming the centerpiece of the room.

DÉCOR

Keep knick-knacks and clutter to a minimum. Home accessories such as vases look less noticeable when they're made of clear glass, and floating photo frames give a more minimal appearance to any hanging artworks.

DEVIL'S IVY
(A.K.A. POTHOS)
Place in bright/indirect sunlight.
Can live in water or soil.
Water regularly, when soil is dry, without soaking the soil.

SOIL: Well-draining potting mix.

FERTILIZER: Houseplant fertilizer, twice per month in summer, once per month in winter.

HOUSEPLANTS

Plants make a space feel like home. Depending on your interior's color scheme, decluttering and reducing your possessions to the absolute minimum can sometimes result in spaces that look stark and unfinished, but plants are a magic solution for making a space feel warm and inviting—and they have the added benefit of bringing fresh air into your home. Try these easy-to-care for varieties.

GOLDEN CANE PALM
(A.K.A. ARECA PALM, YELLOW PALM, OR BUTTERFLY PALM)
Place in full sun and in a large pot. Water before soil becomes dry. Add water crystals to soil (they release water slowly so you don't have to water as often).

SOIL: Rich, moist soil.

FERTILIZER: Mulch, compost, or all-purpose plant food once per month.

HINDU ROPE (A.K.A. INDIAN ROPE PLANT, WAX PLANT, OR HOYA)
Place in bright light.
Water infrequently, as this plant prefers dry conditions.

SOIL: Well-draining and slightly acidic.

FERTILIZER: All-purpose fertilizer during warmer months.

MONSTERA DELICIOSA
(A.K.A. SPLIT-LEAF PHILODENDRON, SWISS CHEESE PLANT, OR WINDOWLEAF)

Place in indirect sunlight. Water regularly; leaves should stay upright if plant has enough water.

SOIL: Most soils are fine.

FERTILIZER: All-purpose fertilizer during warmer months.

ZZ PLANT (A.K.A. ZAMIOCULCAS ZAMIFOLIA, ZANZIBAR GEM, OR ETERNITY PLANT)

Don't overwater. Don't leave soil dry for too many days, either, although this plant can tolerate drought. Place in soft sunlight. Grows best in warm temperatures.

SOIL: All-purpose potting mix.

FERTILIZER: All-purpose fertilizer during summer.

FIDDLE-LEAF FIG

Place in bright, indirect light. Water regularly. Keep moist, but not soaking wet, as too much water will cause root rot. Wipe dust from leaves so the plant receives adequate sunlight.

SOIL: Any fast-draining potting soil.

FERTILIZER: Weak liquid fertilizer during warm months.

SUCCULENTS

Many varieties exist. Place in bright sunlight. Barely water.

SOIL: Shallow, well-draining soil.

FERTILIZER: All-purpose fertilizer during warm months.

CACTI

Many varieties exist. Place in bright sunlight. Barely water.

SOIL: Shallow, well-draining soil.

FERTILIZER: All-purpose fertilizer during warm months.

SNAKE PLANT (A.K.A. MOTHER-IN-LAW'S TONGUE)

Blooms unpredictably, when root-bound; its extremely fragrant flowers smell wonderful. Place in indirect sunlight. Water infrequently (very little water in winter).

SOIL: Well-draining soil.

FERTILIZER: Feed with all-purpose fertilizer.

20 ESSENTIAL
KITCHEN TOOLS

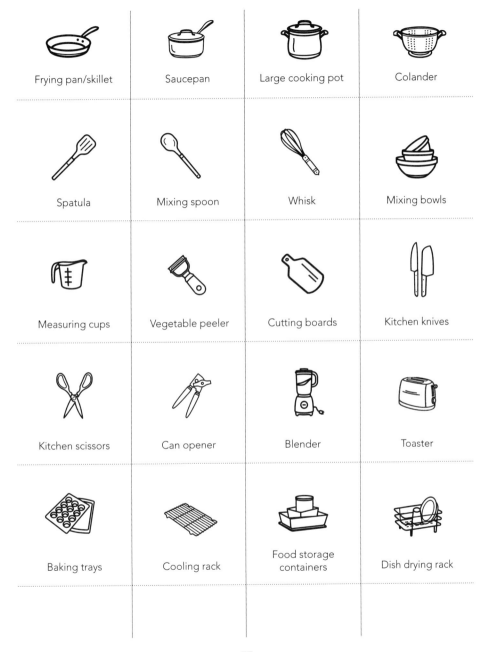

Frying pan/skillet	Saucepan	Large cooking pot	Colander
Spatula	Mixing spoon	Whisk	Mixing bowls
Measuring cups	Vegetable peeler	Cutting boards	Kitchen knives
Kitchen scissors	Can opener	Blender	Toaster
Baking trays	Cooling rack	Food storage containers	Dish drying rack

PANTRY BASICS

When it comes to simplifying your pantry, there are a few things to consider: Who do you have to feed? Do you have a specific diet that you follow? And how often are you eating home-cooked meals? These factors will all impact what kind of staples you should keep.

STORAGE

Opt for glass storage containers. They keep your food fresh and help the pantry look organized. Having them also allows you to purchase in bulk. Buying dry goods and fresh fruit and vegetables in bulk not only saves you money but also reduces the amount of packaging waste that's coming into your home. Think about how much plastic your food is wrapped in when you buy pre-packaged produce from the supermarket! Now you're taking some tiny steps to reduce waste as well as being a bit more frugal with the weekly grocery bill.

MINIMAL **CHALLENGE** *Remove all unhealthy food from your cupboards*

Most pantries will benefit from containing these healthy options, which can create a large variety of meals (in combination with your fridge essentials, of course).

Almond flour
Coconut flour
Almond meal
Oatmeal
Nuts
Nut butters
Seeds
Chia seeds
Stevia/sweetener
Vanilla extract
Dark chocolate
Baking powder
Olive oil
Vinegar
Apple cider vinegar
Broth/stock
Black beans
Lentils
Chickpeas
Quinoa
Brown rice
Polenta
Buckwheat
Psyllium husk
Himalayan salt
Herbs/spices
Garlic
Tea

SIMPLIFY THE COOKING PROCESS

Now it's time to streamline your cooking. This involves ways to cut down on cooking time and the waste that commonly comes with food. It doesn't mean that you have to cut out heaps of ingredients. In fact, aim to keep your meals nutritious so they nurture your body. (The more ingredients, the greater the chances of getting as many types of vitamins as possible.)

MEAL PREPPING

Instead of purchasing a pre-packaged lunch when you're at work, do meal prep. This means cooking three to seven days worth of food at one time, and storing it in the fridge and freezer. Not only will this approach enable you to eat more healthy options throughout the day, it will also save you money. It will also let you recycle any extra plastic and cardboard your ingredients are packaged in (because it's often less effort to just throw away disposable containers when you're at work).

You can meal prep once or twice a week, depending on whether you want to store food in the fridge, freezer, or both. It's best to purchase glass containers for this, because most plastic containers don't last as long. Look for meal prep videos on YouTube. They generally cover a variety of meals you can make for the week, and shopping lists for what you'll need to pick up at the store.

For meal prep, use containers that are reusable, stackable, BPA free, microwavable, and dishwasher safe.

INGREDIENT PREPPING

If you're not ready to fully prep all your meals, a simpler option is to just prep ingredients.

You might have meat marinating for a meal later in the week, for example, and a container of pre-chopped vegetables ready to go in the fridge. That way, when you're short on time in the evening, you can just throw the ingredients into a pan. With no further prep required, your meal will be ready quickly.

If you don't want to prep all your main dishes, a different option is to simply prep all your snacks for the next few days. That way, you won't fall off track from eating well between meals, and you won't be purchasing products in disposable packaging. Some great ideas include sliced veggies and dips, pre-made smoothie ingredient packets, and healthy home-made muesli bars.

USE WHAT YOU HAVE

Another way to simplify the cooking process is by being resourceful with what you have. Stop bringing new ingredients into your pantry! Instead, look through the items you've already got on hand and declutter your kitchen by making dishes from those. Besides, not making a grocery run will save you time.

Soups and curries are perfect for this approach; to make these it's good to always have stock, curry powder, coconut milk, and spices on hand. For example, use up all your leftover vegetables by throwing them into a pot with bone broth to make a yummy, gut-repairing soup. Or if you've got eggs and cheese, combine them with an assortment of whatever vegetables and spices you have on hand to make a filling breakfast frittata.

61

Have nothing in your house that you do not know to be useful, or believe to be beautiful.

—William Morris (1834–1896), textile designer, poet, and socialist activist

THE BEDROOM

Being minimalist doesn't mean suffering from a stark, cold, and uninviting bedroom. Rather, it should feel tranquil and like the perfect place for you to wind down after a long day. If you're in the process of furnishing your space, pick out simple décor items for yourself. If your room is already furnished, start by doing your regular decluttering throughout the room to ensure it doesn't contain large amounts of stuff lying around that you no longer want or need.

HEADBOARDS

A very simple, unobtrusive bedframe won't appear to overwhelm the room.

PILLOWS AND CUSHIONS

Two pillows per person, maximum, and a bare amount of toss pillows or bolsters—or for true minimalism, none at all.

ACCESSORIES AND ACCENT PIECES

Don't go overboard with these; they can unintentionally make a room look far more cluttered than it actually is.

Instead of having a full vanity setup, apply your makeup in the bathroom.

Use clothing racks to display your minimalist wardrobe, or keep garments put away for a neater appearance.

To keep nightstands clutter free, keep reading materials narrowed down to your absolute favorites. Better yet, opt for digital reading whenever possible.

Do you really need a TV if you only stream online and could use your laptop for the same purpose? Consider what other items you actually use and get rid of the rest.

ADOPT KEYSTONE HABITS

A keystone habit is one—or a few—habit(s) that trigger other successful ones to flow in after them. The best place to start these practices is in the space where you sleep, because you can accomplish a few in the morning upon awakening to set yourself up for a successful day. This might include opening the blinds to make the space feel light and airy, or making the bed so that you feel inclined to keep the rest of your space neat, too.

Examples of keystone habits outside the bedroom include:

Exercising each morning, which results in being more conscious of what you eat.
Planning your day and week, which results in getting more done.
Creating and sticking to a financial plan with savings, which reduces clutter and frivolous spending.

THE BATHROOM

The bath can easily become a hot spot for clutter and unused items, especially when many people live together! It's an area that we don't spend long periods of time in, so it often gets a bit neglected when it comes to keeping an eye on what's accumulating and in turn decluttering. Here are some tips to keep your bathroom minimal.

CHECK THE CABINETS

Dig through the medicine cabinets, drawers, and all storage. Remove any expired or unused items, from skincare to old soaps to medication you no longer need to expired makeup.

KEEP SURFACES CLEAR

Keep all the horizontal surfaces in the bathroom as free as possible, except for items that you use daily. This makes cleaning the bathroom easier, and keeps things a lot more hygienic!

TOWELS

Use towels a few times before you throw them in the wash. It will radically cut down your laundry. (This rule doesn't apply to guest towels, obviously.) Using smaller towels allows you to fit more into one wash load.

KEEP THE MESS IN CHECK

Set some simple cleaning habits to ensure the bathroom never gets out of control. This could include wiping down glass shower doors after every use, quickly wiping down the tap and sink after washing your hands or brushing your teeth, and hanging towels immediately after use (this also cuts down on laundry, because towels will smell fresh longer and won't need as frequent washing).

REASSESS PURCHASES

While you're at the store, ask yourself if you really need to stock up on seven tubes of toothpaste just because they're on sale. Is it worth the space you'll lose?

MINIMAL CHALLENGE *Clean out your junk drawer.*

MINIMALIST SKINCARE

Bathroom cabinets can become a mecca of half-used serums, expired cleansers, and nearly empty deodorants. It's time to pull everything out of the cabinets and drawers and declutter your skincare. This will enable you to hang on only to the products that you know actually look after your skin, freeing up space and keeping things looking tidy. Your skincare routine doesn't have to be overly complicated; it just has to work for *you*.

By the way, it's a good idea to consult a skincare specialist to find out what products will work for you. Even though skincare professionals have sales targets to hit and may advise you to get multiple products, their knowledge is more specialized than that of sales assistants in department stores and they'll be able to give you the advice you need.

To declutter, put *all* your skincare products in a pile. Pick each one up in turn and ask yourself these questions.

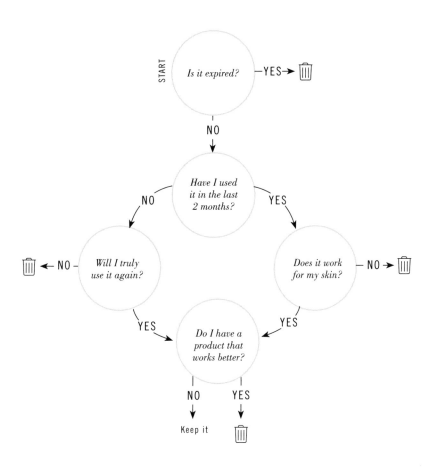

START

Is it expired? —YES→ 🗑

NO ↓

Have I used it in the last 2 months?

NO ↙   YES ↘

🗑 ← NO — *Will I truly use it again?*   *Does it work for my skin?* — NO → 🗑

YES ↘   YES ↙

Do I have a product that works better?

NO   YES
↓   ↓

Keep it   🗑

MINIMALIST MAKEUP

Makeup is not a necessity, so if you want to be ultra minimal, you could get rid of it altogether. But many minimalists do enjoy wearing it, even if it's not every day.

Once you've got a good skincare routine and a healthy diet in place, you'll be able to get by with less makeup. Just a good foundation, or base, will do wonders. For those of you who want to glam themselves up every now and again, here's a list of makeup essentials with the ability to create a large number of versatile looks—not just everyday makeup.

MINIMAL CHALLENGE *Spend the day without any makeup on.*

A **primer or moisturizer,** depending on your skin type: primer for oily skin, and moisturizer for dry.

A **concealer** matched to your skin tone.

A **sheer foundation.** This helps coverage look natural rather than caked on.

Translucent powder for setting.

A **liquid highlight.** This gives a more natural-looking glow.

Mascara. Use it instead of false lashes or heavy eye makeup.

Lip balm, to keep your lips moisturized.

A **colored lipstick,** scarlet red or whatever shade you like.

A **liquid or pencil eyeliner,** for days when you want your eyes to make a statement.

A limited **eyeshadow palette.** Neutrals really work best.

Lip/cheek tint, to use as both a natural lip color and a blush.

Bronzer. It lends a natural glow, or can be used to lightly contour.

Makeup brushes. You can get away with having just these four: a foundation brush, a powder brush, a blending brush, and an eyeshadow brush.

COMMANDMENTS
FOR A TIDY HOME

Reduce the packaging you bring home. Choose products encased in less packaging and avoid single-serving sizes. Buy stuff second-hand.

Refuse shopping bags when you're out, and place all your purchases—books, clothing, sheets, you name it—in your own bag or under your arm.

Shop at grocery stores that don't provide bags, and/or stores that sell foods in bulk to avoid bringing extraneous waste into your house. Bring your own totes to carry purchases home.

Never buy bottled water.

Make your own cleaning products.

Don't purchase produce that's packaged in plastic bags or clamshells, and avoid putting loose produce in produce bags.

Leave the cheap, brittle hangers that some clothing is sold on at the store. Invest in high-quality coat hangers that resist breaking, and that won't stretch your clothing.

Sort your mail and recycle all non-sensitive, unimportant items before bringing the mail into the home.

Whenever possible, refuse paper receipts. Have them emailed to yourself instead.

Sign up for electronic bank statements, bills, and pay stubs.

Don't pick up flyers or brochures. Instead, take a snapshot.

Read newspapers and magazines online or at the library.

DAILY	Set a timer and tidy up for 20 minutes per day.	Immediately make your bed upon waking each morning.	Pick up as you go, don't handle objects twice (see box), move objects where they belong.	Remove your shoes when entering the home to avoid bringing any messes inside.
WEEKLY	Regularly and ruthlessly tidy and organize surfaces in your home.	Caring for clothing allows you to buy less of it. Iron, hang, or fold all clean items. Repair damaged ones.	Put extra thought into every purchase (even the weekly groceries). Do you really need it?	Learn to recycle, and reduce any and all packaging you bring into your home.
MONTHLY	Declutter a problematic area or zone of the house; do this regularly.	Sort through all receipts and paper documents, photograph them, and recycle them.	Let go of things.	Discard redundant items. (You don't need six plain black T-shirts; one will do just fine.)
YEARLY	Set goals and visualize how you'd like your home to feel and look.	Clear out and reorganize storage areas (cupboards, garage, etc.).	Reassess your furniture. Is each piece necessary, or is it merely filling space?	Establish a new rule for how you bring new objects into your home, e.g., one in = one out.

AVOID HANDLING OBJECTS TWICE

Put items away immediately, rather than dropping them thoughtlessly, then having to move them again later. For example, don't initially drape your coat over a chair—hang it.

distilled water

vinegar

hydrogen peroxide

baking soda

salt

lemon essential
oil

tea tree oil

THE ONLY 7 CLEANING PRODUCTS YOU NEED

Making your own cleaning products helps the environment by reducing the amount of artificial products and packaging you're contributing to the landfill, *and* it will also save you money. Your main investment will be in essential oils, which you can purchase online or find in health food stores.

DISENFECTANT =

2 cups (473 ml) warm distilled water (120°F/50°C) + ½ cup (118 ml) vinegar + 30 drops tea tree oil + 15 drops lemon essential oil

GLASS CLEANER =

3 cups (710 ml) vinegar + 1 cup (237 ml) warm distilled water (120°F/50°C) + 15 drops lemon essential oil

DRAIN CLEANER =

15 drops lemon essential oil + ¼ cup (75 g) table salt + ¼ cup (75 g) baking soda + 2 cups (473 ml) boiling distilled water (200°F/90°C)

AIR FRESHENER =

3 tbsp (24 g) baking soda + 2 cups (473 ml) cool water (60°F/16°C) + 15 drops lemon essential oil
Place it in a spray bottle to spritz whenever desired.

STOVE AND OVEN CLEANER =

½ cup (150 g) table salt + 3 tbsp (24 g) baking soda + 3 tbsp (44 ml) vinegar + 3 tbsp (44 ml) warm distilled water (120°F/50°C)

TOILET BOWL CLEANER =

½ cup (118 ml) hydrogen peroxide + 15 drops tea tree oil + ½ cup (118 ml) vinegar + 1 cup (237 ml) warm distilled water (120°F/50°C) + 4 tbsp (32 g) baking soda

ALL-PURPOSE SURFACE CLEANER =

15 drops tea tree oil + ¾ cup (177 ml) vinegar + 3 cups (710 ml) warm distilled water (120°F/50°C)

CLEANING STRATEGIES FOR THE HOME

Cleaning a space is easy, but *keeping* it clean is where many people struggle. Don't fall into a cycle of performing huge cleanups followed by months of mess. By adhering to this checklist, you'll easily keep your home looking pristine all year. You don't have to spend your days scrubbing—it's as simple as completing a few small tasks on a regular basis.

DAILY

- Clean dishes and sink right after eating
- Wipe down table and kitchen surfaces
- Wipe down shower and bathroom surfaces
- Quickly sweep or vacuum floors
- Take out trash
- Clean toilet bowl

WEEKLY

- Thoroughly clean surfaces: bedside tables, dressers, desks, hall tables, etc.
- Laundry, as needed
- Thoroughly mop and scrub floors
- Scrub all bathroom surfaces and toilet
- Clean windows and any glass doors
- Clean microwave and oven
- Clean out fridge
- Change bed sheets and other linens
- Clean floors in patio or outdoor areas
- Clean surfaces in outdoor areas

MONTHLY

- Clean out pantry
- Thoroughly clean appliances: dryer, kettle, washing machine, dishwasher
- Clean mattress
- Clean ceiling fans and vents of air conditioners
- Clean under large furniture: fridge, couch
- Clean curtains and out-of-sight areas like tops of cupboards
- Clean lights and light switches
- Clean doors and door handles
- Clean exterior of windows and doors (doesn't apply to apartments)

YEARLY

- Scrub walls
- Clean out freezer
- Clean gutters
- Clean fireplace and chimney

HOW TO CLEAN...

A dryer: *Wipe the barrel and clear out the lint catch.*

The kettle: *Boil out the lime scale.*

A washing machine: *Run an empty load with vinegar and baking soda.*

The dishwasher: *Remove and soak the filter, mix roughly equal parts vinegar and baking soda together in a saucer, place it in the bottom of the appliance overnight, then scrub it with an old toothbrush.*

Mattresses: *Remove the cover, vacuum any invisible debris, then sprinkle a layer of baking soda over the mattress. Leave it undisturbed for several hours to absorb any excess liquids or oils from on/in the mattress, then vacuum up the baking soda.*

Ceiling fans: *First wipe the top and sides of the fan blades with a cloth soaked in warm water—to catch all the dust without dropping it onto the furniture below—then pass a dry cloth over the blades.*

Air conditioner: *Wipe vents down with a wet cloth. For air conditioner units, remove the cover to access the vents.*

Curtains: *Take down fabric curtains and hand wash them. Wipe down Venetian blinds and roller blinds with a microfiber cloth.*

Light bulbs and lamp shades: *Wipe them with a dry cloth.*

Light switches: *Rub them with a melamine foam pad (such as White Magic Eraser Sponges) to remove marks.*

Doors and door handles: *Activate a melamine foam pad (like White Magic Eraser Sponges) with water and rub away fingerprints and dirt.*

DECLUTTERING THE BASEMENT, ATTIC, & GARAGE

Three of the biggest accumulation zones: the basement, the attic, and the garage. Because they're basically out of sight (and therefore out of mind), these areas of the home are hot spots when it comes to storing unused, broken, or forgotten items. For that reason, they may take a little longer to declutter than more frequented areas of the home.

Use this decision tree to figure out what to keep and what to jettison. Your basement, garage, and attic will also stay more manageable in the long run if from now on you ask yourself the same questions *before* automatically storing stuff in there.

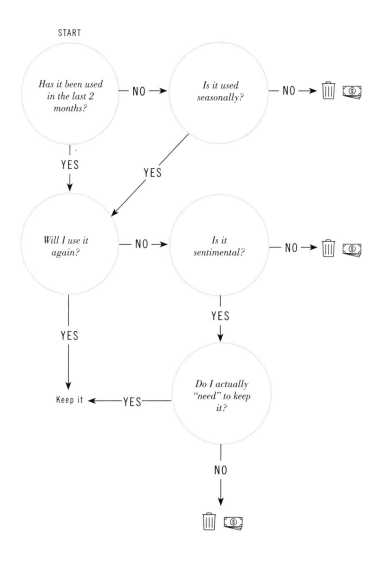

START

Has it been used
in the last 2
months?

— NO →

Is it used
seasonally?

— NO → 🗑 💵

YES

YES

Will I use it
again?

— NO →

Is it
sentimental?

— NO → 🗑 💵

YES

YES

Keep it ← YES — Do I actually
"need" to keep
it?

NO

🗑 💵

MINIMAL CHALLENGE *Declutter your craft/hobby supplies.*

PETS AND KIDS

Children and pets bring a great amount of joy into our lives, but we do need to keep some extra objects around the house to take care of them, and that's okay. Here's how to make sure things don't get out of hand.

ASSIGN A SPACE LIMIT

For kids' toys, set aside a toy box, shelf, or other storage unit as the only place to keep toys. For pets, select one drawer that holds food, leads, treats, grooming supplies, and toys. Once things no longer fit in that space, add nothing to it unless something else goes.

STAY REALISTIC

How many toys do they actually need? You may buy something extravagant only to find they're more interested in playing with the cardboard box it came in … think before you buy. When pets or kids get bored with a toy, put it away for several months, then reintroduce it. They may regain interest.

BE SPECIFIC ABOUT GIFTS

This can be tough with kids, but for birthdays and holidays, ask relatives to purchase something your kids can wear, something they really need, or something educational.

CHANGE TRADITIONS

Adult family members can avoid purchasing gifts for each other altogether. At Christmas, you might all pool together funds. Each person nominates a charity; then draw the winning cause out of a hat and send the money to it. Another option could be for everyone to do a "secret Santa" so each person receives only a single present instead of multiples gifts.

DONATE

When your children grow out of old clothes or no longer use something, donate it to another parent who could put it to better use. (This doesn't apply to pets.)

ALTERNATE ACTIVITIES

Think of other things to do with your pets and children. It's great to have downtime when they're occupied with another activity, but when you're with them, *really* spend your time actually being present with them.

A CURATED
CLOSET

What a funny thing—it's usually the people with overflowing wardrobes who claim, "I have nothing to wear!" An overabundance of less-than-perfect choices makes us feel like we have no options at all. It's now time to curate your closet. A well-designed wardrobe will allow you to feel confident and smartly dressed every day. You'll assemble it to suit your lifestyle and your personal taste, rather than adhering to short-term trends.

DETERMINE YOUR STYLE

Your clothes reflect what's important to you and give the world an insight into your personality and tastes. What do you like, and what do you want to project? In figuring out your style, consider your favorite colors and materials, and what kind of silhouettes complement your body or add edginess to your outfits.

You may have too many clothes, reflecting every trend that has caught your eye. While decluttering now, and while shopping in the future, you'll aim to pare your look down to one overarching style. Here's how.

1. Gather inspiration by finding fashion photos you like on blogs, magazines, and social media.

2. Use those images to help define the overall theme of your style. What do you see the most of? Write down three defining words that come to mind when you envision your ideal wardrobe.

EXAMPLES OF STYLES

Minimal
Casual
Preppy
Glamourous/sexy
Sporty
Bohemian
Classic/chic
Artsy
Business
Sophisticated/polished
Rocker
Goth
Girly
Feminine
Tomboy
Western/cowgirl
Vintage

3. Next, chart your lifestyle. How many hours a week do you spend on various activities? Knowing this will help you figure out not just what you "want" to wear, but what you "need" to wear, and how much of the appropriate clothing you need.

SAMPLE LIFESTYLE PIE CHART

This pie chart maps roughly how many hours per week someone might spend doing the following activities. Do the same for yourself.

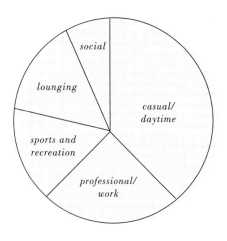

4. Define your key color palette. Grab a box of crayons, get some paint chips, or look at color swatches on your computer—then pick five shades plus one type of metal—gold, silver, brass, or copper.

KEY COLOR PALETTE

Once you've collated all this information and know what single style you'd like your wardrobe to reflect, you'll be ready to start decluttering your closet.

HOW TO CULL YOUR WARDROBE

It's important to look at your closet as a whole and to think of it as an environment where many pieces need to work together, rather than focusing on individual garments that you may like but that may not work well as part of a cohesive and functional wardrobe.

Put on every garment in turn. Snap a photo, review it, and also look at yourself in a mirror, and answer the questions in the decision tree on the opposite page as you do.

Also make sure to keep only the pieces that stick to the style you've determined to be yours. Be firm and honest with yourself, and keep your resolve!

> *In order to cull your wardrobe you'll need a few things:*
>
> - *Four trash bags or cardboard boxes, labeled keep, alter, sell/ donate, throw out*
>
> - *A full-length mirror*
>
> - *A camera or phone to photograph your outfits so you can see how they look from a proper perspective, not just in the mirror.*

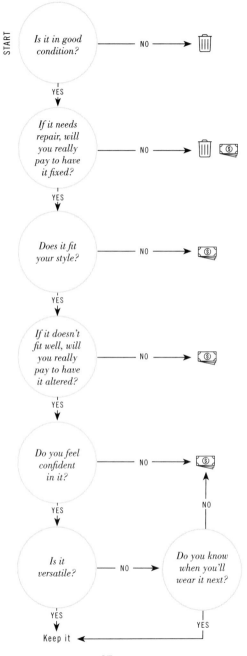

START

Is it in good
condition?
NO →

YES ↓

If it needs
repair, will
you really
pay to have
it fixed?
NO →

YES ↓

Does it fit
your style?
NO →

YES ↓

If it doesn't
fit well, will
you really
pay to have
it altered?
NO →

YES ↓

Do you feel
confident
in it?
NO →

YES ↓

Is it
versatile?
NO →

Do you know
when you'll
wear it next?

NO ↑

YES ↓

YES

Keep it ←

QUALITY OVER QUANTITY

It's crucial to shop for quality over quantity. By investing in fewer high-quality pieces for your wardrobe, you'll end up saving money over the long run, you'll take better care of the pieces you do own, and you won't be contributing to the fast fashion which ends up in the landfill every day. You'll treasure the one garment that you truly love and have worked hard to get for far longer than a throwaway item.

TIPS FOR ASSESSING QUALITY

Take a long, careful look at garments you're considering buying. Keep in mind that a high price tag doesn't always mean quality.

Fuss over fabrics

- Better-quality fabrics are easier to clean and last longer.

- Learn the feel of a good fabric. Cottons should feel thick yet soft against the skin. Denim should never feel thin or flimsy. And cashmere should be sturdy when new, and develop softness over time.

- Synthetic fibers such as acrylic, Spandex, and rayon can decay quickly.

Do the twist   Hold the garment by the top. Does it hang oddly, as if warped? This indicates that it wasn't cut properly.

Search seams   Check the seams—are they well put together? Do they meet properly?

Closing time   Make sure all zippers, buttons, buttonholes, hooks, snaps, etc., are well secured and work properly.

Check the linings   Jackets and coats should have a high-quality lining; a poor lining, or none at all, is indicative of cost-cutting measures.

TIPS FOR REDUCING QUANTITY

Use the following tips to make sure you're only purchasing only the clothing you need.

Before shopping, delineate what you're looking for

- Is your wardrobe missing a certain element?
- What will be the most versatile piece to fill this gap?

Be ruthless

- "Almost" and "not quite" aren't good enough. Don't buy it!
- Does it make you feel amazing, or just okay? Only buy amazing pieces.
- Do you absolutely love everything about it? If not, leave it on the rack.

Simplify

- Look for clothes with less embellishment.
- Versatile pieces will fit with more outfits.

Move to the slow lane

- Where possible, look for locally made garments and designers.
- Slow fashion designers will release fewer collections per year, unlike fast-fashion outlets that have 10 new styles a week (usually stolen from small designers).

CAPSULE WARDROBES

A capsule wardrobe is compact, and contains only essential items that are long-lasting and won't go in and out of fashion with trends. These basic pieces will all work well together, both in terms of styles and colors, and will pair with seasonal items and dress up or down to suit many occasions. Having a capsule wardrobe will simplify your life immeasurably. Turn the page for an example.

CAPSULE WARDROBE

A capsule wardrobe contains a limited number of coordinating clothes that you mix and match to form numerous outfits to suit any occasion. Keeping the colors to two neutrals—black, white, or gray—plus one other shade will make even a small set of items quite versatile.

- You choose the number of items, but less is more.
- Nine items can net you nine outfits.
- You'll typically need more tops than bottoms.
- If well chosen, two pairs of shoes should be enough.
- Layering helps outfits look different from each other.
- Use accessories to change up the look.
- You can update your capsule wardrobe each season, if desired, but keep the same limited amount of garments.

FOR WOMEN

FOR MEN

Buy less. Choose well. Make it last.

—Vivienne Westwood (b. 1941), contemporary fashion designer

20 ESSENTIAL ITEMS FOR SPRING/SUMMER

You may find it hard to believe, but you really don't need more than one of each item on this list. Do note, however, that the list doesn't include underwear, socks, ties, jewelry, accessories, or athletic wear. Each piece should be in the style and colors you detemined earlier for yourself, so that all items work well together.

WOMEN	MEN
Plain white short-sleeve T-shirt	Plain white T-shirt
Tank top	Plain black tee
Short-sleeve top (different cut than T)	Henley top
Button-up blouse, any style	Short sleeve button-up top
Knit sweater	Button-up dress shirt
Day dress	Crewneck sweater
Evening dress	Chinos
Casual shorts	Knee-length pants (casual)
Dress shorts	Slacks
Skirt	Jeans
Lightweight trousers	Tailored suit
Jeans	Lightweight jacket
Light jacket	Windbreaker
Lightweight transitional coat	Casual shoes
Flat shoes	Casual sneakers
Heels	Derbys/dress shoes
Sandals (or open shoes)	Slides (open shoes)
Sunglasses	Sunglasses
Hat	Hat
Bathing suit	Swimwear

20 ESSENTIAL ITEMS FOR AUTUMN/WINTER

Other than a few accessories and standard essentials such as underwear, socks, and athletic gear, you really don't need any more than one of each item on this list. Again, make sure each piece conforms to the style and color scheme you detemined for yourself earlier, so they'll all work together.

WOMEN	MEN
Plain white long-sleeve T-shirt	Plain shirt
Neutral long-sleeve top	Casual long-sleeve top
Colored or dark long-sleeve top	Colored or patterned dress shirt
Button-up blouse	Neutral button-up dress shirt
Fitted sweater	Hoodie
Slouchy sweater	Sweater
Hoodie	Blazer
Simple dress	Suit
Evening dress	Trousers
Long trousers	Chinos
Sweatpants	Sweatpants
Leather jacket	Leather jacket
Heavy winter coat	Heavy coat
Ankle boots	Casual sneakers
High boots	Dress shoes
Sneakers	Derbys/brogues
Slip-on casual shoes	Boots
Hat	Hat
Gloves	Gloves
Scarf	Scarf

ACCESSORIES

Now that you see how few pieces go into a capsule wardrobe, you may wonder if you'll look like you're always wearing the same thing. No, provided you switch things up with accessories. You don't need to own 50 pairs of sunglasses; a few high-quality items will do the trick. Accessorizing outfits incorporates your own personal flair and makes it seem like you have far more than you actually do. It also alleviates any boredom with your wardrobe.

Here's a curated list of mostly unisex accessories for you to add to your outfits to help create different looks. If you want to incorporate color without owning heaps of clothing, accessories are a great way to add a pop of color into a versatile monochromatic wardrobe and brighten up the look. So feel free to deviate from your color palette—except where jewelry is concerned, in which case you should stick to the metal color you selected.

MINIMAL CHALLENGE *Purge one bag of clothing from your closet and donate it.*

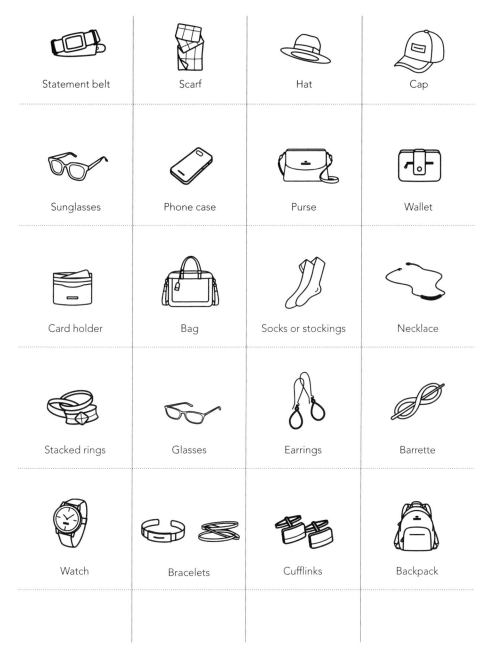

Statement belt	Scarf	Hat	Cap
Sunglasses	Phone case	Purse	Wallet
Card holder	Bag	Socks or stockings	Necklace
Stacked rings	Glasses	Earrings	Barrette
Watch	Bracelets	Cufflinks	Backpack

HOW TO STORE CLOTHES

1

Hang your most-commonly used clothes on the wardrobe rack for easy use. Choose hangers that won't stretch or damage your clothing.

2

Fold and store casual and/or workout clothes on shelves or in drawers.

3

Keep shoes in a dry area. Include a moisture absorber if they're in an enclosed space.

4

Keep bags together in one place and out of the way of general foot traffic to minimize damage.

5

Wardrobe items can be put on display. Use an open clothes rack, for example, or hang hats up on hooks on the wall. This will also protect them from damage.

6

Keeps the laundry basket where there is open air to avoid odor.

7

Store out-of-season items in vacuum bags so as to take up less space.

TIPS FOR REDUCING YOUR LAUNDRY

Wearing clothing that's all in a similar color palette allows you to do less segmented washing.

Wait until you have a full load to wash.

If you only wore something for an hour or so, it probably doesn't need to be washed. Overwashing can wear down fabrics.

Use towels for a week instead of washing them after every use.

SIMPLIFY YOUR LIFE

There's more to minimalism than just the amount of stuff you own, or how much you're able to get rid of. Truly adopting minimalism will benefit your mental clarity, your budgeting, and even the flow of daily living. Learning to simplify your life will allow you to identify what's really important to you, and give you the time to focus on those things.

CLARIFYING GOALS

Minimalism hacks away at the non-essentials, and schedule clutter is one of these. Once you've eliminated the clutter from your schedule, you'll have more time to put toward your goals and to focus on what you'd truly like to spend energy on. Eliminate unnecessary tasks so you can grow your career, spend more time with your family, or enjoy your hobbies.

Start by deciding what's important to you. We do need sleep and downtime, and we have to switch off every now and again. We're only granted a limited number of hours in a day, and can't juggle *everything* into place. Accept that you can't do everything on your own.

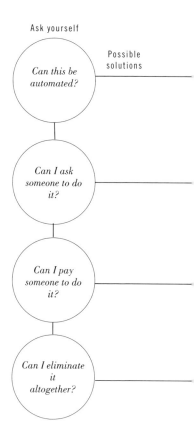

Ask yourself

Possible solutions

Can this be automated?

Can I ask someone to do it?

Can I pay someone to do it?

Can I eliminate it altogether?

	GOAL	DUE DATE	TRACKING METHOD
SHORT-TERM GOAL #1 (1 month)			
SHORT-TERM GOAL #2 (4 month)			
SHORT-TERM GOAL #3 (7 month)			
LONG-TERM GOAL (12 month)			

SIMPLIFYING YOUR COMMITMENTS

After listing your goals, look at your schedule with the aim of crossing clutter off it. As you consider each task, check to see if it meshes with your goals, and refer to this flowchart.

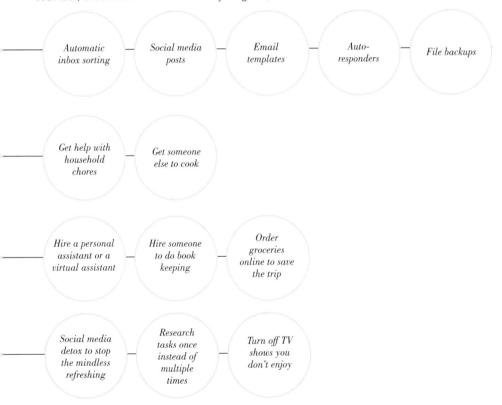

10 WAYS TO SINGLE-TASK

Juggling tasks, dividing your attention, and trying to accomplish too many things at once has actually been proven to be counter-productive. Accomplishing your to-do list to the best of your ability and in an efficient timeframe is best done by completing one item at a time. Here are 10 methods to become more productive and learn the art of single-tasking.

1   EAT WITHOUT YOUR PHONE

This may seem like a very basic concept, but you'd be surprised at how many times you try to check your phone when it's not around. Focus on your food and be thankful for it.

2   SET A TIMER

Using a timer when you're studying or working can help you single-task more efficiently. For example, set yourself a 25-minute window to study, followed by a five-minute break; repeat.

3   WRITE IT DOWN

Instead of being distracted by your looming mental checklist, write a comprehensive to-do list at the start of the day.

4   USE ONLY ONE BROWSER TAB

Rather than flicking between all the different tabs you have open, attempt to get your work done using a single tab. This allows you to really focus on what you're doing.

5 CURB DISTRACTIONS

Within the limits of what you're capable of, control your distractions. This may mean shutting yourself in a room away from your dogs or noisy housemates, putting up "do not disturb" signs, and logging out of social media.

6 TURN ON AIRPLANE MODE

If you have work to get done, switch your phone to airplane mode so you can't access the internet or social media.

7 ASSIGN TIMES

Where possible, allocate yourself times purely to do one task. For example, start your day with 20 minutes of sorting through and organizing your email inbox, and do no other tasks during that time.

8 TURN OFF THE EXTERNAL NOISE

If you're really struggling to stay focused, make sure there's no music playing in the background, and no TV on to distract you.

9 READ OR WATCH TO COMPLETION

If you're watching a movie or show, or reading an article, finish doing so in one sitting. Practice being able to get through the whole article or show without breaking your concentration.

10 REFOCUS

If you do slip up while single-tasking, don't just give up. Refocus, figure out why it went wrong, and attempt to avoid that distraction next time if possible.

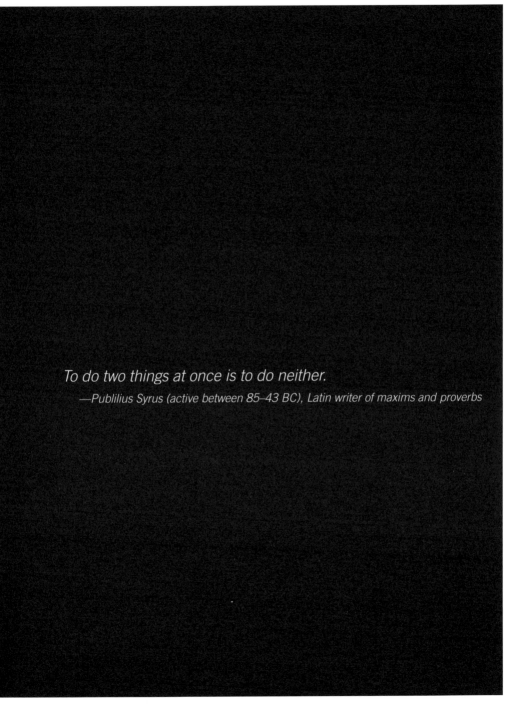

To do two things at once is to do neither.
—Publilius Syrus (active between 85–43 BC), Latin writer of maxims and proverbs

SPENDING INTENTIONALLY

Spending intentionally doesn't mean you have to live life on a budget so restrictive that it doesn't allow for play or enjoyment. It's about figuring out how to pay for the things you need first, putting aside savings at the same time, and after that allocating funds for pleasure. Small daily expenditures toward things that don't benefit you in the long run will begin to add up and work against you and your budget.

MINIMAL CHALLENGE *Determine whether your last 10 purchases were intentional.*

THERE'S NO ONE-SIZE-FITS-ALL PLAN

When it comes to spending intentionally, everyone has different expenses and also different pleasures. Some people enjoy spending a small amount of their income on books, while others prefer to purchase experiences to remember. After making sure that your bills and a small amount of savings (or a large amount, if it's within your means) are covered, dedicate a portion of money to yourself to actually enjoy your life—and be grateful for what you can do. What you choose to buy in life should bring some kind of pleasure to your existence and to those around you. Maybe this means that you'll treat yourself to fine chocolates, maybe you'll go to the movies, or maybe you'll book a skydiving trip.

WAIT TO SPEND

Cutting unnecessary spending allows you to utilize your money on more important things. Think of the junk you purchase and never use, or the expensive coffee drink you buy but could have brewed at home. So before you spend on something you're not sure you actually need, make sure to stop, breathe in, and take a different action that will help you remember the item for later (bookmark it on your computer, take a photo of it on your phone, or write a list)—but don't buy it now! Wait at least a week, then see if you still want it.

MAKING A BUDGET & STAYING ON IT

A budget is essentially your roadmap to financial success. Many people are able to get by without one, but when you don't have a budget in place it's hard to plan for future investments, or even emergencies. Having a budget may sound tedious or stressful to some, but wouldn't you prefer to know where your hard-earned money is actually going?

Don't set up a budget as a way to restrict and stop yourself from spending altogether. Rather, it's a method for planning future financial success and making sure your money isn't going toward things you no longer use or weren't even aware that you were spending on. In order to start your budget, take these steps.

THE PROCESS

1 Determine your income

Know exactly what you have available monthly, after taxes.

2 Savings or repayment goals

Set your monthly savings goal (or a goal for paying off loans or credit cards) and set up an automated transfer from your bank account each week or month to accomplish this goal.

3 Track one or two months of expenses

You can do this using bank statements. For cash, keep a journal or some kind of filing system for receipts. There are also multiple apps that can help with this.

4 Categorize

Next, organize all of your expenditures into groups: food, bills, insurance, travel, clothing, loan repayments, etc.

5 Observe what needs to change

Notice some peculiar spending habits? Could you perhaps reduce your extravagant grocery expenditures, or maybe that phone bill that runs over each billing period? And how does your spending compare to your income? It may be time to set some limits, such as a set amount for activities or dining out each month.

6 Implement change

Based on what you've observed, start to knock down the overspending.

TRIAL AND ERROR

Test-drive your new budget for two to three months, then repeat the entire process to see if you were able to stick to it or whether you need to work on cutting down more expenses.

EFFECTIVE SHOPPING HABITS

When you're trying to live life as a minimalist, you should not subscribe to the concept of shopping as a hobby or entertainment. You shop strictly because you need something, not to kill time. Here are ways to buy far less.

SET TIME LIMITS *BEFORE* PURCHASING

Many of the things we buy are actually impulse purchases. If you spot something you want, instead of buying it now, make a note 10 days away in your calendar. On that day, you can decide whether you still want it as badly as you thought you did.

SET A MONTHLY BUYING LIMIT

Track the amount you've spent daily, and stick to the limit you've set. Think of it as a game. And if possible, pay with cash rather than a card. It's psychologically harder to part with real money than to whip out plastic.

RID YOURSELF OF TEMPTATIONS

Unsubscribe from store emails, and call catalog companies to have them remove you from their mailing lists. Avoid shopping centers and malls.

STICK TO YOUR GUNS

Make lists of the things you need—not want, but *need*—and purchase nothing else.

BUYING GARMENTS

Clothing is especially tempting to many shoppers. Keep these points in mind.

Don't buy if …

- You haven't waited 10 days.
- You already own something similar that's in good shape.
- You want it just to impress someone.
- You can't afford it.
- You're only buying because it's on sale.
- You're bored and want something new.
- You only like it for the brand name.
- Its sole purpose is to make you feel better.
- You hope the item will motivate you to exercise or lose weight.
- The item is high maintenance and you're unwilling to iron it or pay for dry cleaning, for example.

After waiting 10 days, buy it only if …

- You actually *need* it.
- You still absolutely love it in every way.
- You own nothing else like it.
- It's of high quality and will last.
- It works with the rest of your wardrobe.
- You know what other item you'll relinquish in order to bring this new one in (see the one-in/one-out system).
- You'll wear it often.
- You don't need anything else to complete the garment (the right pants, for example).

INSTEAD OF BUYING …

Consider renting or borrowing special-occasion clothing for one-time events like awards, ceremonies, or wedding receptions.

ORGANIZING YOUR TIME

By organizing your time, you'll not only be able to create a more sustainable work/life balance for yourself, but you'll learn to start incorporating more time for hobbies and relaxation into your week. With minimalism in mind, seek to free your schedule from any unnecessary tasks or things you don't find enjoyable, so you can in turn focus on what's important in your life. This could mean making more time to exercise for health, spending time with family, or taking some down time for yourself. Incorporate these four methods into your scheduling.

USE A CALENDAR

Track all upcoming tasks. From meetings to dinner with friends to entertainment to flight times and names, put as much in there as you can. That way, when you check for an overview of your day you have as much detail as you need in one place.

BREAK YOUR DAY INTO BLOCKS

Segment the day into blocks to get the most out of it. Some of these blocks might be "Work," "Gym," or "Family time." This way, each of your primary focuses—tasks that you *have* to do, e.g., work and tasks that you gain a lot of enjoyment from such as date night or workout time—will have dedicated time.

USE A TO-DO LIST

To break down your day further and ensure you can complete the tasks you need to within the allotted "blocks," write yourself a to-do list. This could be in an app on your phone, a shared list with a partner, or just a list kept in a journal. Set tasks for each day in a notebook or phone to ensure that they're all done; if they're not, move them to the next day.

SCHEDULE TIME OFF

For any workaholic, scheduling time off is a must! You need to make sure to get the rest and recuperation your body needs to function at its best during working hours.

PLANNING YOUR SCHEDULE

Planning is the best way to make sure you actually stick to your intentions when it comes to time organization. You can opt to use a mobile calendar app, an appointment app, a journal, or a planner. Planning daily maximizes how much you're able to get done and ensures you're not filling your time with "clutter."

Here's an example of how to structure and segment a day to get the most done.

5:00	Wake up
5:00–6:00	Get ready/breakfast/cleaning
6:00–7:30	Gym
7:30–8:00	Free time/commute
8:00–11:00	Work
11:00–12:00	Update social media/lunch
12:00–4:00	Work
4:00–5:30	Free time/commute/walk/dinner
5:30–7:30	Work
7:30–10:30	Relax

MINIMAL CHALLENGE *Wake up 30 minutes earlier.*

DECLUTTERING YOUR DIGITAL SPACE

The digital realm is often overlooked when it comes to decluttering, but it can make a tremendous impact on how efficiently you use your devices! Think of how often you're on your computer or phone, navigating your way through a million vacation pictures (or photos of beloved pets), searching for that one document that you named in some random manner because you were in a hurry, rather than what it needed to be called so you could find it easily. It's time to declutter the virtual! Just because you can't see digital files as physical clutter in a room doesn't mean things aren't getting messy.

TIDY UP YOUR COMPUTER

Follow these steps, in order, once every two weeks to ensure files don't get out of control.

1. Clear everything off the desktop

2. Organize the filing system
   - Name files correctly
   - Place files in appropriate folders and subfolders
   - Back up files
   - Empty the downloads folder
   - Empty the trash
   - Clean up the disk

3. Sort through applications
   - Remove any you don't use
   - Delete any duplicates

4. Organize bookmarks
   - Arrange them into folders
   - Remove any you no longer need

5. Tidy up your inbox
   - Use only one mail application
   - Unsubscribe from marketing emails
   - Apply automated inbox segmenting—tags, subfolders, and inbox sorting automation. (Once set up, this sorts emails into categories and folders, such as work, personal, or any others you define, based on the preferences you set up, such as the sender or keywords in the email.)

6. Social media
   - Unfollow irrelevant organizations or people
   - Unfriend unsuitable people or organizations

TIDY UP YOUR PHONE

Complete the following tasks in this order once a month to keep your phone organized.

1. Organize apps, then clear your home screen
   - Create folders on your phone home page to place all apps into. Folders might include "social media," "photography," "life" (for the calculator, alarm, etc.), and "other" (random apps you can't uninstall).
   - Delete any you don't use
   - Delete any duplicate or similar apps

2. Remove all media
   - Delete unnecessary photos and videos
   - Back up all photos and videos you wish to keep onto your computer
   - Delete all photos and videos from phone
   - Turn off cloud sharing

3. Clear out your contacts
   - Delete all unnecessary contacts
   - Delete all messages
   - Set messages to automatically expire after 30 days

4. Tidy up your calendar
   - Unlink unused calendars
   - Delete unnecessary birthdays and holidays

5. Notifications
   - Choose which to leave on and which to turn off

DIGITAL DETOXING

Unplugging from technology—is that a scary thought for you? If so, that's perhaps even more reason to give it a try. A digital detox is simply giving yourself a break from all of your digital devices at once. You may find this experience very conflicting and uncomfortable at first, and you'll undoubtedly check your (switched-off) phone often.

HOW TO DIGITALLY DETOX

Completely turn off your phone.

Don't open your laptop, pad, or computer.

Keep the TV off.

No video games.

Read a print book, not an eBook.

Turn the music off.

Take off your Apple watch or its equivalent.

MINIMAL CHALLENGE *Take an entire day completely off the internet.*

Over an extended period of time, short breaks from electronics and social media can improve your mood, mental well-being, and even your sleep! Many people aren't fully aware of how much time they waste endlessly scrolling through the vast abyss of social media.

It's up to you what kind of break suits your lifestyle, especially if your job requires electronics and an internet connection. Your boss probably wouldn't be jazzed if you turned up for work and said, "Oh, sorry, I'm having a digital detox day."

You may need to schedule in the digital detox. It could involve taking one whole weekend completely offline, or it may only be possible to do partially, by not getting online until the afternoon of a single day. It might just mean all electronics (TV, phone, etc.) stay off during meal times only.

At first you'll need to adjust to the nagging feeling of needing to check your phone or messages, but once you overcome this, you can be far more productive. A digital detox allows your brain to calm down and relax while it's not being inundated with media.

CREATING A MINIMALIST WORKSPACE

4

CATCHALL

A small, elegant box can store items before they become clutter—but keep the container small, and put away everything in it at the end of each day.

5

CHANGE YOUR FILING SYSTEM

If you end up with papers everywhere, file them in drawers or folders. Or digitize your filing to avoid wasting paper.

6

CLEAR OUT DRAWERS

Empty all storage, and refill only with essentials.

7

TIDY UP

Take five minutes at the end of each day to push in your chair and tidy up your workspace. This creates a pleasant environment to come work in next time.

8

STAY GREEN

A plant livens up the workspace.

9

INSPIRATION

An inspiration board of images or an inspirational quote can refresh your workspace and make it feel more personalized.

10

CIRCULAR FILING CABINET

Toss out everything you don't need right away.

1

FIGURE OUT WHAT YOU NEED

Consider what essentials the workspace actually requires. Do you really need a printer that you only use once every few months?

2

REDUCE CLUTTER

Reassess all knickknacks and clutter. Do they actually serve a purpose?

3

CLEAR YOUR DESK

Take everything off your desk; only add back what you strictly need.

GRATITUDE JOURNALING

The simple act of writing down the things you're grateful for can reduce your stress levels, result in better sleep, and increase your overall happiness. Taking the time to harness a reflective mindset and focus on all the positives in your life on a regular basis will help you recognize what's important to you, and help steer your focus toward those things.

WHAT IS GRATITUDE JOURNALING?

Keeping a gratitude journal is a way to keep track of all the things you're thankful for in your life. This could be anything from the warm weather to your pets, or even a delicious breakfast.

WHY SHOULD YOU DO IT?

Studies have shown that spending a small amount of time each day reflecting on some things you appreciate and creating a headspace of thankfulness and happiness increases the overall well-being of the people who do it. When it comes to minimalism, being thankful for what you already have will help you focus on what you've got rather than grumbling about what you wish you had.

HOW DO YOU DO IT?

All you need is a notebook or journal. Every day, set aside five to 15 minutes to write down some things you're grateful for. Don't just roll through the motions and write down things because you "have to," as if it were a chore. Really focus and think about them.

Writing an A-to-Z gratitude list is an interesting method. Start by writing all the letters of the alphabet. Beside each, write something you're deeply grateful for that starts with that letter.

21-DAY SELF-CARE CHALLENGE

DAY	TO-DO
1	Read a book for fun.
2	Cook yourself a healthy meal.
3	Go for a walk.
4	Eat no processed foods.
5	Meditate.
6	Get eight hours of sleep.
7	Completely log off social media.
8	Try a new hobby.
9	Find new music.
10	Go for a hike.
11	Spend the day only single-tasking.

DAY	TO-DO
12	Plan a weekend vacation (or a staycation).
13	Stay offline.
14	Treat yourself to a massage or an at-home spa day.
15	Spend at least two hours outside.
16	Plant something.
17	Practice mindful breathing for 20 minutes.
18	Do nothing at all today.
19	Plan a fun day with a friend.
20	Try something new.
21	Spend 30 minutes stretching or doing yoga.

STAYING MINIMAL LONG-TERM

Now that you've decluttered, culled, and reorganized, your space feels refreshed and looks more open, and you're probably feeling a bit more clarity, too! Now it's time to establish methods and habits to ensure you'll keep in place your new lifestyle and your tidy home. This chapter offers tips that you can use to make sure your house, wardrobe, and mind don't ever get as cluttered as they were before.

DON'T PROCRASTINATE

Procrastination is at the core of the failure to move forward with where you want to be in life. Instead of scrolling through social media endlessly, you could be finishing off that degree at a faster rate or working on a creative project you feel passionate about. Delaying things and putting them off will only make them seem larger and more frightening when you do finally get around to doing them. Follow these easy tips to avoid procrastination.

LESS-THAN-A-MINUTE RULE

For any task that can be done in less than one minute (replying to an email, putting your shoes away instead of leaving them out when you get home, wiping the sink, etc.), do it immediately.

WORST = FIRST

Do the tasks you enjoy the least at the first opportunity. This gets them out of the way and you won't have to think about them anymore.

FILE MAIL AND DOCUMENTS

Sort documents immediately to drastically reduce clutter. This also includes paying bills immediately to avoid late fees.

SET GOALS

Write a list of what you'd like to accomplish each day so you're able to track how much you've achieved.

REWARD PROGRESS

Allow yourself a reward for getting a certain amount of tasks done for the day. Maybe it's relaxing and watching an episode of your favorite show, pampering yourself in some way, or treating yourself to that chapter of a book you've been meaning to finish.

ONE IN/ONE OUT SYSTEM

After sorting through your items, decluttering, and establishing what does and doesn't suit your lifestyle, you need to avoid accumulating again. The one in/one out system is a tried-and-true way to keep clutter controlled and avoid repurchasing unnecessary items.

WHAT IS ONE IN/ONE OUT?

Each time you purchase and bring a new item into your home, you must purge one thing you already own in return.

This system requires a great deal of discipline and practice. You must remember to not procrastinate; remove the unwanted item immediately and you'll be successful with the one in/one out method.

IS ONE IN/ONE OUT TIT FOR TAT?

You don't necessarily have to apply the method to items of a similar nature, but that's the easiest place to start. So, for example, if you bought a shirt, you might jettison an existing shirt. However, you could instead get rid of pants—or a book, mug, or appliance.

CHOOSING WHAT TO PURGE

While buying less is the best option, applying the one in/one out system should help avoid the overflow of clutter, which would in turn force you to have to repurge what you own over and over again. Once you've bought a new item, ask yourself the questions in the chart at right to help find an existing item to purge.

Or better yet, answer the questions in the flow chart on the opposite page *before* you buy anything new. If you have nothing to purge, purchase nothing.

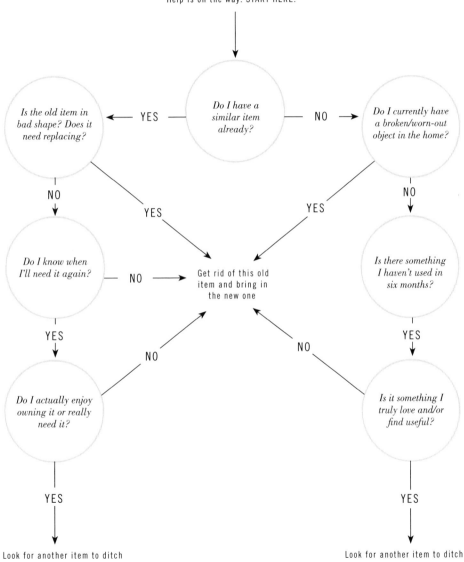

You have a new item and need to get rid of something else to bring the fresh one into your space—but you can't figure out what to ditch. Help is on the way. START HERE:

Do I have a similar item already?

YES → Is the old item in bad shape? Does it need replacing?

NO → Do I currently have a broken/worn-out object in the home?

Is the old item in bad shape? Does it need replacing?
NO → Do I know when I'll need it again?
YES → Get rid of this old item and bring in the new one

Do I know when I'll need it again?
NO → Get rid of this old item and bring in the new one
YES → Do I actually enjoy owning it or really need it?

Do I actually enjoy owning it or really need it?
NO → Get rid of this old item and bring in the new one
YES → Look for another item to ditch

Do I currently have a broken/worn-out object in the home?
YES → Get rid of this old item and bring in the new one
NO → Is there something I haven't used in six months?

Is there something I haven't used in six months?
YES → Is it something I truly love and/or find useful?

Is it something I truly love and/or find useful?
NO → Get rid of this old item and bring in the new one
YES → Look for another item to ditch

NO-SPEND DAYS

Instituting no-spend days can reinforce the habit of being more responsible with your money. It doesn't mean not to pay your bills. It simply means not to purchase anything you don't really need. Make your coffee at home in the morning rather than buying a cup while you're out, don't make that online clothing purchase, and avoid last-minute grocery runs.

NO-SPEND DAYS ONE-MONTH CHALLENGE

Next month—or, heck, start right now—transfer these seven no-spend days to your calendar and buy nothing on them. It's easier than you think!

SUNDAY	MONDAY	TUESDAY	WEDNESDAY	THURSDAY	FRIDAY	SATURDAY
				✕		
	✕					
			✕			✕
		✕				
	✕			✕		

137

WISH LISTS

Creating wish lists is a highly effective way to stick to your newly created budget, or to manage your spending.

KEEP IT STRAIGHT

Create three separate lists to help you track what you need versus what you want. Name one "need," the next "want," and the last one "wish."

Need

This is for items that you need soon.

Want

Under "want," list items or experiences you want that are within your means.

Wish

The "wish" category lists any purchase you want to make that's currently beyond your means; this could perhaps be a large investment of some sort.

Whichever way you create your wish list (see ideas at right), keep any item in that list for a minimum of 30 days before you take action to purchase it. (Of course, this applies only to items that don't have a time limit on them, such as tickets to see your favorite band or some other activity you'd like to partake in, or items in your "need" list.)

VARIOUS WAYS TO MAKE WISH LISTS

Keep a written list

Go old school.

Bookmark

Wish lists can be as easy as bookmarking products you'd like to buy in your browser.

Photograph

Take a photo of the item in a shop and add it to your phone's "favorites" photo album. This will help you remember it.

LIVING WITH A NON-MINIMALIST & MAKING IT WORK

It's all well and good for you to go ahead with a minimal lifestyle, but what if the person you live with wants nothing to do with it? You can't force it on others, and you definitely shouldn't declutter for them—that's a great way to make someone resent the lifestyle and maybe even hold a grudge against you. So here are some tips for living with non-minimalists to make a space that you can both share and enjoy.

LEAD BY EXAMPLE

No matter what lifestyle choice you've made, don't impose it on someone else.

MAKE A GAME OF IT

For example, suggest a challenge like "remove five things each week" and share this job with the person or people you live with.

COMPROMISE

If the people you live with feel there's an item they absolutely must have in their lives, let them have it. You can't have total control over communal spaces.

PERSONAL SPACE

Find a space in the house that you can keep as minimal as you like, and others should have a space in the house they can keep as cluttered as they want.

ORGANIZATION

If they don't want to declutter and it's really annoying you, just talk about it! See if you can help the other person organize the space to look neater.

Edit your life frequently and ruthlessly. It's your masterpiece after all.

—Nathan W. Morris, contemporary financial coach, author, and speaker

Penguin
Random
House

Publisher Mike Sanders
Associate Publisher Billy Fields
Senior Editor Nathalie Mornu
Book Designer Rebecca Batchelor
Photographer Rachel Aust
Illustrator Rachel Spoon
Proofreader Laura Caddell

First American Edition, 2018
Published in the United States by DK Publishing
6081 E. 82nd Street, Indianapolis, Indiana 46250

Copyright © 2018 Dorling Kindersley Limited
A Penguin Random House Company
21   10 9 8 7 6 5
008–309804–June/2018

ISBN: 978-1-4654-7350-9
Library of Congress Catalog Number: 2017956777

DK books are available at special discounts when purchased in
bulk for sales promotions, premiums, fund-raising, or
educational use. For details, contact: DK Publishing Special
Markets, 345 Hudson Street, New York, New York 10014 or
SpecialSales@dk.com.

Printed and bound in China

All images © Dorling Kindersley Limited
For further information see: www.dkimages.com

for the curious
www.dk.com

ABOUT THE AUTHOR

With a background in fashion and beauty photography, Rachel Aust began her YouTube career in 2015 as a way to explore her creativity through videography and share her passion for minimalism and organization. Also holding degrees in nutrition and fitness and the owner of a fitness brand, Rachel likes to promote healthy well-being, both of the body—through fitness—and also of the mind—via minimalism. She believes in living life at your fullest potential and ridding yourself of distractions, both mental and physical, in order to achieve that. Through minimalism, Rachel has been able to create her ideal home environment, reduce stress, and also share her journey with others.